D0039528

The Modern Spirituality Series

Thomas Merton

The Modern Spirituality Series

The Modern Spirituality Series

Thomas Merton

A selection of his writings
edited by Aileen Taylor
with an introduction by Monica Furlong

TEMPLEGATE PUBLISHERS

First published in 1988 by
Darton,Longman & Todd Ltd., London
Arrangement © 1988 Aileen Taylor
Introduction © 1988 Monica Furlong

Published in 1990 in the United States by
Templegate Publishers
302 East Adams St./PO Box 5152
Springfield, IL 62705

ISBN 0-87243-174-6
Library of Congress catalog card number 89-52146

The cover photograph of Rene Magritte's
"The Tempest" is reproduced
with the permission of the Wadsworth Atheneum,
Hartford, Connecticut. Bequest of Kay Sage Tanguy.

Contents

Acknowledgement

The editor and the publishers are grateful to the Merton Legacy Trust for their co-operation in making this book of daily readings possible.

Introduction

I have loved Thomas Merton ever since a day in 1968 when I sat down and read an essay of his called *The Cell*. (I had read him long before this, when *Elected Silence* and its successors were published in England, but in those days found him grim and life-denying. The 'new' Merton had undergone some inner revolution that I longed to learn about.) If it is true that we fall in love with what we are trying to find, or realize, or complete, in ourselves, then I think I would want to point to Merton's developed sense of paradox, to his ability to live with contradiction, to his willingness to struggle with the realities of the world (instead of living in a Christian ghetto), and finally, to his passion for union with God which was a dominant concern during most of his adult life.

Paradox and contradiction were built into Merton's family background. Merton was born in France in 1915 to a New Zealand father and an American mother. He was educated in France, America and England. This, together with the fact that his mother died when he was six and his father when he was fourteen (and that he spent most of his early life being moved around among relatives and guardians or away at boarding-school), meant that he had little sense of 'belonging'. Although he was loved – in particular by his grandparents – he lacked all continuity of care, and seemed to feel, more even than most of us, an emotional hunger, a painful inner emptiness that nothing quite filled. His youthful remedy for

11

this was a fierce activism as he threw himself, to the point of exhaustion and beyond, into whatever life offered – rugger, practical jokes, languages, art, literature, travel, love. At his English public school he detested the absence of girls. Years later he was to say that in adolescence he had needed someone to fall in love with, and there was no one. He filled his study with pin-ups of Hollywood stars and learned about women and love through literature – in particular through Hemingway and Lawrence.

The rigidity of boarding-school, little as he enjoyed it, had perhaps spelled a kind of security for a disturbed adolescent. Cambridge, on the other hand, offered a bewildering and rather melancholy freedom. Merton did little academic work, and was continually in trouble for excessive drinking and for climbing in and out 'after hours'. Much more seriously, he 'got a girl into trouble'. When he returned to America to visit his grand-parents for the summer vacation his English godfather suggested that he should not return.

At Columbia, where he completed his education, he suffered a minor breakdown, but managed to pull his life into some kind of shape. He came under the influence of an inspired English teacher, Mark Van Doren, he formed new and important friendships (in particular with Robert Lax), he flirted briefly with Communism but was drawn, largely by the philosophy of Jacques Mari-tain, to Catholicism. He was received into the Catholic Church in 1938, and almost at once formed a simultaneous longing to be ordained priest and to enter a religious Order. In 1941, at the age of twenty-six, he applied to and was accepted by the Order of Cistercians of the Strict Observance (the Trappists). Their house was in a lonely stretch of country near Bardstown in Kentucky.

At the time that Merton entered the Order the régime was very severe. Except in interview with superiors the monks never spoke, but communicated with one another in sign language. Their day began at two in the morning when they left their dormitories and began the long cycle of daily prayer in the church. Six to eight hours a day of prayer, pious reading, heavy manual work (the monks ran a substantial farm), household chores, kept the monks busy from morning till night. Food was sparse. In a climate that is intensely hot and humid in summer and bitterly cold in winter, the monks had neither air-conditioning nor heating and often found themselves wearing their thick woollen cloaks on a boiling summer's day.

Yet the life had distinct joys – a basic simplicity that appealed very much to Merton, an intense awareness of the natural world and of the seasons, a spiritual spaciousness. To begin with, it offered a great relief from the exhausting multiplicity of choices he had known outside; perhaps, too, from a nagging sense of guilt. Gethsemani, as the monastery was called, did not lack penances.

Inevitably, however, unresolved neurotic conflicts returned, more especially after Merton had been ordained priest. He was assailed by panic attacks when he had to say Mass, or even to read aloud. He began to suffer from permanent exhaustion and from many physical complaints. A spell of rest and proper nourishment in the local hospital restored him somewhat, yet the disturbance did not go away.

Merton had already begun to make a name for himself as a writer before he entered the Order, contributing to the *New Yorker* and to small magazines. In his scant spare time at Gethsemani he wrote an account of the life that had led him to Christian conversion and to the monastery, and at the instigation of his Abbot, Dom Frederic, the manuscript was sent to a New York publisher, Robert Giroux of Harcourt Brace. Published in 1948 as *The Seven-Storey Mountain*,* it amazed everyone by becoming a bestseller. Tucked away in the isolation of his monastery Merton had, paradoxically, become famous. He was both excited and appalled.

Dom Frederic was replaced as Abbot by Dom James, a rigorist with whom Merton was to cross swords on a number of occasions. The writer and contemplative in Merton was growing increasingly distressed at the implacable 'busyness' of Gethsemani, and the lack of solitude. He was permitted two hours a day in which to write, but letters, business matters concerning his books, correspondence with other abbeys, writing abbey publications on demand, had all to be squeezed into this valuable little bit of time. Gethsemani was filling up with novices (some of them, ironically, brought into the monastery by Merton's book) and the enclosure was packed with men. Yet it was forbidden to leave the grounds of the Abbey

*Later published in Great Britain as *Elected Silence*.

14

without permission. It was almost impossible to be alone.

Depressed by these conditions Merton tried to negotiate to join an Order which allowed more solitude, but Dom James would not hear of it. He put Merton in charge of the woods surrounding the Abbey, which gave him more freedom; shortly afterwards Merton became Novice Guardian. He had read widely in the Fathers and was a gifted teacher. In addition to a deep interest in the contemplative tradition of Christianity, he enjoyed the 'family' sense of being responsible for the care of his juniors in the spiritual life. Many of his students have since testified to his wisdom, loving care and insight.

Merton did not confine himself to discussing 'spiritual' topics. In the early days of his life at Gethsemani he had shown a furious contempt for 'the world', and refused to take an interest in it or its ways. But now, with his encouragement, his students discussed the political dilemmas of the modern world, and watched developments with interest; they also read widely in modern literature, in particular some of the literature coming out of South America. Merton himself had begun to read around some of the great issues of the postwar world – to reflect upon the Holocaust, upon the threat of nuclear war, upon the struggle between East and West, upon the American presence in Vietnam. Famous people – Boris Pasternak, Martin Luther King – started to correspond with Merton, and a trail of workers in the Civil Rights Movement and the Peace Movement began to make their way to Kentucky. He struck up new friendships – with Protestants, with Jews, with the famous Zen scholar D. T. Suzuki – with anyone and everyone who was prepared to struggle honestly with the intractable problems of a suffering world. Reading Rachel Carson's *Silent Spring*, Merton became passionately interested in ecological issues.

Gradually, not entirely with Dom James's blessing, Merton had eased himself out of the monastery and into a cinderblock hut in the grounds of Gethsemani where he lived as a sort of hermit. Between letters and visitors it was scarcely a solitary existence, but Merton hugely enjoyed the silent nights, the simple domestic chores, the freedom to write and to pray within his own time-table. When Dom Flavian (one of Merton's former students) became Abbot he gave Merton permission to leave enclosure and make a longed-for trip to the East – to India, Thailand, Japan, and to return home via England. By this stage of his life Merton had a profound interest in Hinduism and, more particularly, in Buddhism. In India he met the Dalai Lama and many other holy men. In Sri Lanka, deeply moved by seeing the huge recumbent figures of the Buddha at Polonnaruwa, he had an extraordinary sense of inner clarity. 'I don't know when in my life I have ever had such a sense of beauty and spiritual validity running together in one illumination . . . I know and have seen what I was obscurely looking for. I don't know what else remains but I have now seen and have pierced through the surface and have got beyond the shadow and the disguise.' Six

16

days later, attending a conference of monks and nuns in Bangkok, he died alone in his room, whether of a heart attack or an electric shock it is not clear. He was fifty-three.

Since Merton's death there have been hagiographic attempts to turn him into a saint, which perhaps is our human way of sealing off remarkable human beings so that we are not forced to learn uncomfortable truths from their inspired originality. We should try to see Merton in a human framework so that we can note carefully what he tells us.

Merton began his time at Gethsemani by hating the world and solemnly warning himself against newspapers, radio and television. Although he never lost sight of the human temptation to fill our loneliness with chattering nonsense, he later perceived that his earlier attitude derived from contempt, from a cold superiority that wished to escape from the human condition. On a shopping trip to Louisville, late in his life, he suddenly knew himself to be one with the people milling about the streets and he rejoiced in this simple discovery:

At the corner of Fourth and Walnut, in the center of the shopping district, I was suddenly overwhelmed with the realization that I loved all those people, that they were mine and I theirs, that we could not be alien to one another even though we were total strangers. It was like waking from a dream of separateness, of spurious self-isolation in a special world, the world of renunciation and supposed holiness

17

... The sense of liberation from an illusory difference was such a relief and such a joy to me that I almost laughed out loud ...

The problem of living alongside other people, he noted, was connected with our fear of losing our identity, our fear that we may not have an identity at all. There is, of course, a sense in which our identities *are* illusory, and the fear that this creates tempts us to pump up a 'false identity' to console ourselves for our sense of nothingness. For Merton the only way to have a true identity is to find ourselves in God's purpose for us, as a flower or an animal does, without fretting or false importance. 'Each particular being, in its individuality, its concrete nature and entity, with all its own characteristics and its private qualities and its own inviolable identity, gives glory to God by being precisely what He wants it to be here and now.'

Another way of coming at the problem is to ask how we bear our loneliness, our sense of cut-off-ness from the world around us. Merton's paradoxical answer to this is 'enter into solitude', embrace the pain of loneliness to the point where we perceive just how illusory it is. Somehow or other, sooner or later, the Christian must voluntarily enter the desert, there to discover that far from being the place of desolation it appears, once the eye gets used to it it is full of extraordinary beauties of its own.

The desert for us, as it was for Jacob, is the place of encounter with God. It is there, says Merton, that we find God, *Qui Est*, the I Am of the burning bush. 'It is as though the Name were waiting in the desert for me, and had been preparing this meeting from eternity and in this particular place, this solitude chosen for me . . . living in the presence of this great Name I gradually become the one He wills me to be.'

Merton's own desert was not, as we have seen, in a bare sandy landscape or even in a city slum, but in the heart of a monastery where he felt alone and miserable, and in a cinderblock hut facing the Kentucky hills. It does not matter what the desert consists of – there are as many deserts as people. What matters is to be present in the place where the meeting is prepared and to take the risk of embracing the experience and entering into the solitude. It is here that there is the chance to 'know God'.

Merton does not underestimate the troubling, baffling effort involved in trying to reach out to God. For a start our minds are accustomed to a kind of knowing – what Merton calls 'the arrogant gaze of our investigating mind' – which does not get us very far. To know God we have to perform a sort of somersault to 'become aware of ourselves as known by him'. This *is* our identity – we 'possess' God in the proportion that we know ourselves to be possessed. What we thought we knew and understood about the world turns out to be fairly useless – so much junk to be jettisoned so that we can embark on the original path to which God summons us. But only as we follow the path do we discover 'who we are'.

In Merton's case the road into solitude led through an intense involvement with the world as

it is and a new involvement with some of its creatures – with the deer and the birds he watched
from the hermitage, with the men under his care,
with women (earlier in his monastic career he had
been unable to see women as themselves, but
merely, in the tragic Christian tradition, as sources
of temptation), with the struggle of the southern
blacks for Civil Rights, and with members of other
religions. Imaginatively, and with inevitable pain,
he entered into the literature of the Holocaust,
and thought and read deeply about what he
regarded as the terrible dangers of our techno-
logical society with its habit of thinking abstractly
about people. He struggled too with the irrevers-
ible damage done to the earth and its creatures.
The callow young man who had once despised
'creatures' had learned a very different lesson.

Yet it was not a grim or joyless progress. What
bubbles through Merton's later letters and sings
through much of his life is a wonderful quality of
lightheartedness, as if he has found a joke that he
can never quite forget. The joke is the sense of the
cosmic Dancer 'playing' through us. 'It is He alone
that one takes seriously. But to take Him seriously
is to find joy and spontaneity in everything, for
everything is gift and grace.'

MONICA FURLONG

The key to the meaning of life

Realization of the Supreme 'Player' whose 'play' is manifested in the million-formed inexhaustible richness of beings and events is what gives us the key to the meaning of life.

Once we live in awareness of the cosmic dance and move in time with the Dancer, our life attains its true dimension. It is at once more serious and less serious than the life of one who does not sense this inner cosmic dynamism. To live without this illuminated consciousness is to live as a beast of burden, carrying one's life with tragic seriousness as a huge, incomprehensible weight.

The weight of the burden is the seriousness with which one takes one's own individual and separate self. To live with the true consciousness of life centered in Another is to lose one's self-important seriousness and thus to live life as 'play' in union with a Cosmic Player.

It is He alone that one takes seriously. But to take Him seriously is to find joy and spontaneity in everything, for everything is gift and grace.

In other words, to live selfishly is to bear life as an intolerable burden. To live selflessly is to live in joy.

Christian asceticism

It is only when we are detached from created things that we can begin to value them as we really should. It is only when we are 'indifferent' to them that we can really begin to love them.

The indifference of which I speak must, therefore, be an indifference not to things themselves but to their effects in our own lives.

The man who loves himself more than God, loves things and persons for the good he himself can get out of them. His selfish love tends to destroy them, to consume them, to absorb them into his own being. His love of them is only one aspect of his own selfishness.

The man who loves God more than himself is also able to love persons and things for the good that they possess in God. Such a man is indifferent to the impact of things in his own life. He considers things only in relation to God's glory and God's will.

We have to be detached from health and security, from pleasures and possessions, from people and places and conditions and things. We have to be indifferent to life itself, in the gospel sense, living like the lilies of the field.

His paradise and our own

All nature is meant to make us think of paradise.
Woods, fields, valleys, hills, the river and the sea,
the clouds travelling across the sky, light and darkness, sun and stars, remind us that the world was
first created as a paradise for the first Adam, and
that in spite of his sin and ours, it will once again
become a paradise when we are all risen from
death in the second Adam.

Heaven is even now mirrored in created things.
All God's creatures invite us to forget our vain
cares and enter into our own hearts, which God
Himself has made to be His paradise and our own.

If we have God dwelling within us, making our
souls His paradise, then the world around us can
also become for us what it was meant to be for
Adam – his paradise.

But if we seek paradise outside ourselves, we
cannot have paradise in our hearts. If we have no
peace within ourselves, we have no peace with
what is all around us. Only the man who is free
from attachment finds that creatures have become
his friends. When he is pure, they speak to him
of God.

God Who owns all things

The Lord God is present where the new day shines in the moisture on the young grasses. The Lord God is present where the small wildflowers are known to Him alone. The Lord God passes suddenly in the wind, at the moment when night ebbs into the ground.

He Who is infinitely great has given His children a share in His own innocence. His alone is the gentlest of loves: whose pure flame respects all things.

God, Who owns all things, leaves them all to themselves. He never takes them for His own, the way we take them for our own and destroy them. He leaves them to themselves.

He keeps giving them all that they are, asking no thanks of them save that they should receive from Him and be loved and nurtured by Him, and that they should increase and multiply, and so praise Him. He saw that all things were good, and He did not enjoy them. He saw that all things were beautiful, and He did not want them.

His love is not like ours. His love is unpossessive. His love is pure because it needs nothing. In Him there is no hunger.

The beauty of all created things

You flowers and trees, you hills and streams, you fields, flocks and wild birds, you books, you poems, and you people, I am unutterably alone in the midst of you.

The irrational hunger that sometimes gets into the depths of my will, tries to swing my deepest self away from God and direct it to your love. I try to touch you, but I cannot touch you, and I am abashed, solitary and helpless, surrounded by a beauty that can never belong to me.

But this sadness generates within me an unspeakable reverence for the holiness of created things, for they are pure and perfect and they belong to God and they are mirrors of His beauty.

He is mirrored in all things like sunlight in clean water: but if I try to drink the light that is in the water I only shatter the reflection.

And so I live alone and chaste in the midst of the holy beauty of all created things, knowing that nothing I can see or hear or touch will ever belong to me, ashamed of my absurd need to give myself away to any one of them or to all of them.

Conversion

There is a conversion of the deep will to God that cannot be effected in words – barely in a gesture or ceremony. There is a conversion of the deep will and a gift of my substance that is too mysterious for liturgy, and too private.

It is something to be done in a lucid secrecy that implies first of all the denial of communication to others except perhaps as a neutral thing.

I shall remember the time and place of this liberty and this neutrality which cannot be written down. These clouds low on the horizon, the outcrops of hard yellow rock in the road, the open gate, the perspective of fence-posts leading up the rise to the sky, and the big cedars tumbled and tousled by the wind. Standing on rock. Present.

The reality of the present and of solitude divorced from past and future. To be collected and gathered up in clarity and silence and to belong to God and to be nobody else's business.

I wish I could recover the liberty of that interior decision which was very simple and which seems to me to have been a kind of blank check and a promise.

A new humanism

We are called to create a better world. But we are first of all called to a more immediate and exalted task: that of creating our own lives.

In doing this we act as co-workers with God. We take our place in the great work of mankind, since in effect the creation of our own destiny, in God, is impossible in pure isolation. Each one of us works out his own destiny in inseparable union with all those others with whom God has willed us to live.

We share with one another the creative work of living in the world. This active response, this fidelity to life itself and to God Who gives Himself to us through our daily contacts with the material world, is the first and most essential duty of man.

Christianity does not teach man to attain an inner ideal of divine tranquillity and stoic quiet by abstracting himself from material things. It teaches him to give himself to his brother and to his world in a service of love in which God will manifest his creative power through men on earth.

The center of Christian humanism is the idea that God is love, not infinite power. Being love, God has given himself without reservation to man so that He has become man. It is man, in Christ, who has the mission of not only making himself human but of becoming divine by the gift of the Spirit of Love.

The solitary

In reality, all men are solitary. Only most of them are so averse to being alone, or to feeling alone, that they do everything they can to forget their solitude.

That one who is called to solitude is not called merely to imagine himself solitary, to live as if he were solitary, to cultivate the illusion that he is different, withdrawn and elevated. He is called to emptiness.

And in this emptiness he does not find points upon which to base a contrast between himself and others. On the contrary, he realizes, though perhaps confusedly, that he has entered into a solitude that is really shared by everyone.

It is not that he is solitary while everybody else is social: but that everyone is solitary.

What the solitary renounces is not his union with other men, but rather the deceptive fictions and inadequate symbols which tend to take the place of genuine social unity – to produce a façade of apparent unity without really uniting men on a deep level.

Even though he may be physically alone, the solitary remains united to others and lives in profound solidarity with them, but on a deeper and mystical level.

True fruitfulness

Is it true to say that one goes into solitude to 'get at the root of existence'? It would be better simply to say that in solitude one is at the root. He who is alone, and is conscious of what his solitude means, finds himself simply in the ground of life.

To be as a seed in the ground of one's very life is to dissolve in that ground in order to become fruitful.

To be fruitful one must forget every idea of fruitfulness or productivity, and merely be.

Modern man believes he is fruitful and productive when his ego is aggressively affirmed, when he is visibly active, and when his action produces obvious results.

Solitude is not withdrawal from ordinary life. It is not apart from, above, 'better than' ordinary life; on the contrary, solitude is the very ground of ordinary life.

It is the very ground of that simple, unpretentious, fully human activity by which we quietly earn our daily living and share our experiences with a few intimate friends.

God's will for me

It is all very well to declare that I exist in order to save my soul and give glory to God by doing so. And it is all very well to say that in order to do this I obey certain commandments and keep certain counsels. Yet knowing this much, and indeed knowing all moral theology and ethics and canon law, I might still go through life conforming myself to certain indications of God's will without ever fully giving myself to God.

For that, in the last analysis, is the real meaning of His will. He does not need our sacrifices, He asks for our *selves*.

And if He prescribes certain acts of obedience, it is not because obedience is the beginning and the end of everything. It is only the beginning. Charity, divine union; transformation in Christ: these are the end.

And since no man is an island, since we all depend on one another, I cannot work out God's will in my own life unless I also consciously help other men to work out His will in theirs.

His will, then, is our sanctification, our transformation in Christ, our deeper and fuller integration with other men. And this integration results not in the absorption and disappearance of our own personality, but in its affirmation and its perfection.

Thy neighbour as thyself

How am I to know the will of God?

Whatever is demanded by truth, by justice, by mercy, or by love must surely be taken to be willed by God.

To consent to His will is, then, to consent to be true, or to speak truth, or at least to seek it.

To obey Him is to respond to His will expressed in the need of another person, or at least to respect the rights of others

For the right of another man is the expression of God's love and God's will. In demanding that I respect the rights of another, God is not merely asking me to conform to some abstract, arbitrary law: He is enabling me to share, as His son, in His own care for my brother.

No man who ignores the rights and needs of others can hope to walk in the light of contemplation.

Fanaticism

Faith and prejudice have a common need to rely on authority and in this they can sometimes be confused by one who does not understand their true nature. But faith rests on the authority of love while prejudice rests on the pseudo-authority of hatred.

Everyone who has read the gospel realizes that in order to be a Christian one must give up being a fanatic, because Christianity is love. Love and fanaticism are incompatible.

Fanaticism thrives on aggression. It is destructive, revengeful and sterile. Fanaticism is all the more virulent in proportion as it springs from inability to love, from incapacity to reciprocate human understanding. Fanaticism refuses to look at another man as a person. It regards him only as a thing.

He is either a 'member' or he is not a member. He is either part of one's own mob, or he is outside the mob.

From its very birth, Christianity has been categorically opposed to everything that savours of the mass movement. A mass movement always places the 'cause' above the individual person, and sacrifices the person to the interests of the movement.

For the sake of persons

Contrast this with the teaching of Christ, for whom the soul of the individual was more important than the most sacred laws and rites, since these exist only for the sake of persons, and not vice versa.

Christ even placed the bodily health and well-being of individuals before the law of the Sabbath. One of the bitterest complaints made against Him was that He cured on the Sabbath.

Here is the great temptation of the modern age, this universal infection of fanaticism, this plague of intolerance, prejudice and hate which flows from the crippled nature of man who is afraid of love and does not dare to be a person.

It is against this temptation most of all that the Christian must labour with inexhaustible patience and love, in silence, perhaps in repeated failure, seeking tirelessly to restore, wherever he can, and first of all in himself, the capacity of love and understanding which makes man the living image of God.

Monastic freedom

Monastic discipline and freedom are correlatives. The craving for a certain kind of comfort, reassurance and diversion can be satisfied only if one is willing to accept certain social conditions: to fulfill a prescribed role, to occupy a definite place in society, to live according to acceptable social norms. If we fulfill the role imposed on us by others, we will be rewarded by approval.

These roles impose definite limitations, but in return for accepting the limitations, we enjoy the consolation of companionship, of understanding, support, and so on. We are made to feel that we 'belong' and are therefore 'all right'.

The monastic idea, originally, was to explore the possibilities that were opened up once these limitations were removed, that is to say, once one 'left the world'.

The comforts and joys of ordinary social life, married love, friendly converse and recreation among other people, business, a place in the city and the nation, were to some extent renounced.

It was simply a question of obscurely realizing that, in some, the limitations imposed by social life stood in the way of something else, and the monk was one who wanted to look into this 'something else'.

The inner life

The supposed 'inner life' may actually be nothing but a brave and absurd attempt to evade reality altogether. Under the pretext that what is 'within' is in fact real, spiritual, supernatural, etc., one cultivates neglect and contempt for the 'external' as worldly, sensual, material and opposed to grace.

This is bad theology and bad asceticism. In fact it is bad in every respect, because instead of accepting reality as it is, we reject it in order to explore some perfect realm of abstract ideals which in fact has no reality at all.

Very often, the inertia and repugnance which characterize the so-called 'spiritual life' of many Christians could perhaps be cured by a simple respect for the concrete realities of everyday life, for nature, for the body, for one's work, one's friends, one's surroundings, etc.

A false supernaturalism which imagines that 'the supernatural' is a kind of Platonic realm of abstract essences totally apart from and opposed to the concrete world of nature, offers no real support to a genuine life of meditation and prayer.

Meditation has no point and no reality unless it is firmly rooted in life.

Like other men

My happiness could have taken form in the words: 'Thank God, thank God that I am like other men, that I am only a man among others.'

It is a glorious destiny to be a member of the human race, though it is a race dedicated to many absurdities and one which makes many terrible mistakes; yet, with all that, God Himself gloried in becoming a member of the human race. A member of the human race!

To think that such a commonplace realization should suddenly seem like news that one holds the winning ticket in a cosmic sweepstake.

The conception of 'separation from the world' that we have in the monastery too easily presents itself as a complete illusion: the illusion that by making vows we become a different species of being, pseudo-angels, 'spiritual men', men of interior life, what-have-you.

We are in the same world as everybody else, the world of the bomb, the world of race hatred, the world of technology, the world of mass media, big business, revolution, and all the rest.

We take a different attitude to all these things, for we belong to God. Yet so does everybody else belong to God.

A spring morning

A spring morning alone in the woods. Sunrise: the enormous yolk of energy spreading and spreading as if to take over the entire sky. After that: the ceremonies of the birds feeding in the wet grass. The meadowlark, feeding and singing. Then the quiet, totally silent, dry, sun-drenched midmorning of spring, under the climbing sun.

It was hard to say psalms. Attention would get carried away in the vast blue arc of the sky, trees, hills, grass, and all things.

How absolutely central is the truth that we are first of all part of nature, though we are a very special part, that which is conscious of God.

In solitude, one is entirely surrounded by beings which perfectly obey God. This leaves only one place open for me, and if I occupy that place then I, too, am fulfilling His will. The place nature 'leaves open' belongs to the conscious one, the one who is aware, who sees all this as a unity, who offers it all to God in praise, joy, thanks.

One has to be alone, under the sky, before everything falls into place and one finds one's own place in the midst of it all.

Identity

Each particular being, in its individuality, its concrete nature and entity, with all its own characteristics and its private qualities and its own inviolable identity, gives glory to God by being precisely what He wants it to be here and now.

The special, clumsy beauty of this particular colt on this April day in this field under these clouds is a holiness consecrated to God by His own creative wisdom, and it declares the glory of God.

The pale flowers of the dogwood outside this window are saints. The little yellow flowers that nobody notices on the edge of that road are saints looking up into the face of God.

This leaf has its own texture and its own pattern of veins and its own holy shape, and the bass and trout hiding in the deep pools of the river are canonized by their beauty and their strength.

The lakes hidden among the hills are saints, and the sea too is a saint who praises God without interruption in her majestic dance. The great, gashed, half-naked mountain is another of God's saints. There is no other like him. He is alone in his own character; nothing else in the world ever did or ever will imitate God in quite the same way. That is his sanctity.

The creation

In the beginning, when the Lord created heaven and earth, the Spirit of God moved over the abyss.

There was light. God divided light from darkness. He separated the waters. He called the firmament 'heaven'. He called the stars by their names, and they stood before Him, crying 'We are here!' And they sang together before Him, as Job would hear them sing.

There were seas, there was dry land. Seeds and grass sprang up out of the land. Dolphins played in the waters. Rare birds flew up out of the marshes between the land and the sea. Cries and clear songs filled all the forests, praised Him.

Wild horses ran in their herds like wind upon the prairies. The glades gave up their deer as the leopard came down to the stream to quench her thirst. And where the lion looked up in the long brown grass, a thousand antelopes raced down the bank of the great estuary with their beauty playing in the silent water.

The glory, the strength, the grace, the suppleness, the life of all things came into being at a command from God and praised Him.

Adam – who was to be a 'son' of God

'Then the Lord God formed man out of the dust of the ground and breathed into his nostrils the breath of life, and man became a living being.'*

The life of Adam, that is to say, the 'breath' which was to give actuality and existence and movement to the whole person of man, had mysteriously proceeded from the intimate depths of God's own life. Adam was created not merely as a living and moving animal who obeyed the command and will of God. He was created as a 'son' of God because his life shared something of the reality of God's own breath or Spirit. For 'breath' is the same as 'spirit'.

If the expression may be permitted, Adam's very existence was to be a kind of 'inspiration'. God intended not only to conserve and maintain Adam's bodily life. He would also foster and increase, even more directly and intimately, the spiritual life and activity which were the main reason for Adam's existence.

Adam, then, was meant from the very first to live and breathe in unison with God.

For him, then, to live would mean to 'be inspired' – to see things as God saw them, to love them as He loved them, to be moved in all things ecstatically by the Spirit of God.

* Gn 2:7.

The meaning of existence

One thing above all is important: the 'return to the Father'. The Son came into the world and died for us, rose and ascended to the Father; sent us His Spirit, that in Him and with Him we might return to the Father.

That we might pass clean out of the midst of all that is transitory and inconclusive: return to the Immense, the Primordial, the Source, the Unknown, to Him Who loves and knows, to the Silent, to the Merciful, to the Holy, to Him Who is All.

To seek anything, to be concerned with anything but this is only madness and sickness, for this is the whole meaning and heart of all existence, and in this all the affairs of life, all the needs of the world and of men, take on their right significance.

To 'return to the Father' is not to 'go back' in time, to roll up the scroll of history, or to reverse anything. It is a going forward, a going beyond.

Our destiny is to go on beyond everything, to leave everything, to press forward to the End and find in the End our Beginning, the ever-new Beginning that has no end.

The sense of indigence

The Fathers of the Church saw that every one of us is more or less like the Prodigal, starving in a distant land, far from our Father's House.

This is the common condition of mankind exiled from God and from paradise by an inordinate preoccupation with perishing things and by a constant inclination to self-gratification and sin.

Since this is in fact our position, and since our mental prayer is a journey from time into eternity, from the world to God, it follows that we cannot make a good meditation unless we realize, at least implicitly, the starting-point of our journey.

If we admit the truth, we will start out on a basis of humility, recognize the need for effort, and perhaps we will be rewarded with a little of the grace of compunction, which is the most precious of all helps in mental or any other kind of prayer. Compunction is simply an awareness of our indigence and coldness and of our need for God.

For the man who has a sense of compunction, prayer is a living act which brings him face to face with God in an I–Thou relationship which is not imaginary but real.

Being what we are not

The sin of Adam which robbed him and us of paradise was due to a false confidence, a confidence which deliberately willed to make the option and experiment of believing in a lie.

There was nothing in Adam's perfect peace that warranted this playing with unreality. There was no difficulty in the precept that had to be kept, to avoid falling into illusion. There was no weakness, no passion in his flesh, that drove him to an irrational fulfilment in spite of his better judgment.

All these things would only be the consequence of his preferences for what 'was not'. Even the natural and healthy self-love by which Adam's nature rejoiced in its own full realization could gain nothing by adding unreality to the real. On the contrary, he could only become less himself by being other than what he already was.

All this can be summed up in the one word: pride. For pride is a stubborn insistence on being what we are not and never were intended to be.

Pride is a deep, insatiable need for unreality, an exorbitant demand that others believe the lie we have made ourselves believe about ourselves.

Created to be a child of God

If we are to love sincerely and with simplicity, we must first of all overcome the fear of not being loved. And this cannot be done by forcing ourselves to believe in some illusion, saying that we are loved when we are not.

We must somehow strip ourselves of our greatest illusions about ourselves, frankly recognize in how many ways we are unlovable, descend into the depths of our being until we come to the basic reality that is in us, and learn to see that we are lovable after all, in spite of everything!

This is a difficult job. It can only really be done by a lifetime of genuine humility.

But sooner or later we must distinguish between what we are not and what we are. We must accept the fact that we are not what we would like to be. We must cast off our false, exterior self like the cheap and showy garment that it is.

We must find our real self, in all its elemental poverty but also in its very great and very simple dignity: created to be a child of God, and capable of loving with something of God's own sincerity and His unselfishness.

Rebellious opposition

We are not only contingent beings, dependent on the love and will of a Creator — we are also sinners who have freely repudiated this relationship. We have rebelled against him.

Our 'nothingness' is then something more than the contingency of the creature. It is compounded with the dread of the sinner alienated from God and from himself, set in rebellious opposition to the truth of his own contingency.

The real import of dread is to be sought in an infidelity to a personal demand of which one is at least dimly aware: the failure to meet a challenge, to fulfill a certain possibility which demands to be met and fulfilled.

The price of this failure to measure up to an existential demand of one's own life is a general sense of failure, of guilt. And it is important to remark that this guilt is real, it is not necessarily a mere neurotic anxiety. It is the sense of defection and defeat that afflicts a man who is not facing his own inner truth and is not giving back to life, to God and to his fellow-man, a fair return for all that has been given him.

No easy answers

Let us frankly recognize the true import and the true challenge of the Christian message. The whole gospel kerygma becomes impertinent and laughable if there is an easy answer to everything in a few external gestures and pious intentions.

Christianity is a religion for men who are aware that there is a deep wound, a fissure of sin that strikes down to the very heart of man's being. They have tasted the sickness that is present in the inmost heart of man estranged from his God by guilt, suspicion and covert hatred.

If that sickness is an illusion, then there is no need for the cross, the sacraments and the Church . . . then there is no need to preach Christ any more and there is no need either of liturgy or of meditation.

It is precisely the function of dread to break down this glass house of false interiority and to deliver man from it. Without dread, man would remain content with himself and with his 'inner life' in meditation, in liturgy or in both.

Without dread, the Christian cannot be delivered from the smug self-assurance of the devout ones who know all the answers.

.

Self-denial

It is not complicated to lead the spiritual life. But it is difficult.

We are blind, and subject to a thousand illusions. We must expect to be making mistakes almost all the time. We must be content to fall repeatedly and to begin again to try to deny ourselves, for the love of God.

It is when we are angry at our own mistakes that we tend most of all to deny ourselves for love of ourselves.

We want to shake off the hateful thing that has humbled us. In our rush to escape the humiliation of our own mistakes we run head first into the opposite error, seeking comfort and compensation. If that is all our self-denial amounts to, our mistakes will never help us.

The thing to do when you have made a mistake is not to give up doing what you were doing and start something altogether new, but to start over again with the thing you began badly and try, for the love of God, to do it well.

There is nothing to live for but God, and I am still full of the orchestras that drown His Voice.

Two identities

In becoming man, God became not only Jesus Christ but also potentially every man and woman that ever existed. In Christ, God became not only 'this' man, but also in a broader and more mystical sense, yet no less truly, 'every man'.

The presence of God in His world as its Creator depends on no one but Him. His presence in the world as Man depends, in some measure, upon men.

Not that we can do anything to change the mystery of the Incarnation in itself: but we are able to decide whether we ourselves, and that portion of the world which is ours, shall become aware of His presence, consecrated by it, and transfigured in its light.

We have the choice of two identities: the external mask which seems to be real and which lives by a shadowy autonomy for the brief moment of earthly existence, and the hidden, inner person who seems to us to be nothing, but who can give himself eternally to the truth in whom he subsists.

It is this inner self that is taken up into the mystery of Christ, by His love, by the Holy Spirit, so that in secret we live 'in Christ'.

If I find my true self

Ultimately the only way that I can be myself is to become identified with Him in whom is hidden the reason and fulfilment of my existence.

Therefore there is only one problem on which all my existence, my peace and my happiness depend: to discover myself in discovering God. If I find Him I will find myself and if I find my true self I will find Him.

That is something that no man can ever do alone. Nor can all the men and all the created things in the universe help him in this work. The only One who can teach me to find God is God, Himself, alone. God utters me like a word containing a partial thought of Himself.

If I am true to the concept that God utters in me, if I am true to the thought of Him I was meant to embody, I shall be full of His actuality and find Him everywhere in myself, and find myself nowhere.

To be 'lost' is to be left to the arbitrariness and pretences of the contingent ego, the smoke-self that must inevitably vanish.

To be 'saved' is to return to one's inviolate and eternal reality and to live in God.

My own sanctity

For me to be a saint means to be myself. Therefore the problem of sanctity and salvation is in fact the problem of finding out who I am and of discovering my true self.

Trees and animals have no problem. God makes them what they are without consulting them, and they are perfectly satisfied.

With us it is different. God leaves us free to be whatever we like. We can be ourselves or not, as we please. We are at liberty to be real, or to be unreal. We may wear now one mask and now another, and never, if we so desire, appear with our own true face.

We are free beings and sons of God. We are called to share with God the work of creating the truth of our identity. We can evade this responsibility by playing with masks, and this pleases us because it can appear at times to be a free and creative way of living.

It is quite easy, it seems to please everyone. But in the long run the cost and the sorrow come very high.

To work out our own identity in God . . . demands close attention to reality at every moment. Unless I desire this identity and work to find it with Him and in Him, the work will never be done.

Union with Him

How can I say that I have found Him and found myself in Him if I never know Him or think of Him, never take any interest in Him or seek Him or desire His presence in my soul?

What good does it do to say a few formal prayers to Him and then turn away and give all my mind and all my will to created things, desiring only ends that fall far short of Him?

If my mind does not belong to Him then I do not belong to Him either. If my love does not reach out towards Him but scatters itself in His creation it is because I have reduced His life in me to the level of a formality, forbidding it to move me with a truly vital influence.

Set me free from the laziness that goes about disguised as activity when activity is not required of me, and from the cowardice that does what is not demanded, in order to escape sacrifice.

But give me the strength that waits upon You in silence and peace. Give me humility in which alone is rest, and deliver me from pride which is the heaviest of burdens.

Our awakening

Every moment and every event of every man's life on earth plant something in his soul. For just as the wind carries thousands of winged seeds, so each moment brings with it germs of spiritual vitality that come to rest imperceptibly in the minds and wills of men.

We must learn to realize that the love of God seeks us in every situation, and seeks our good. His inscrutable love seeks our awakening.

Since this awakening implies a kind of death to our exterior self, we will dread His coming in proportion as we are identified with this exterior self and attached to it.

There is an irreducible opposition between the deep, transcendent self that awakens only in contemplation, and the superficial, external self which we commonly identify with the first person singular. We must remember that this superficial 'I' is not our real self.

The 'I' that works in the world, thinks about itself, observes its own reactions and talks about itself is not the true 'I' that has been united to God in Christ.

Contemplation is precisely the awareness that this 'I' is really 'not I' and the awakening of the unknown 'I' that is beyond observation and reflection and is incapable of commenting upon itself.

To refuse everything?

The seeds that are planted in my liberty at every moment, by God's will, are the seeds of my own identity, my own reality, my own happiness, my own sanctity.

To refuse them is to refuse everything: it is the refusal of my own existence and being: of my identity, my very self.

Every one of us is shadowed by an illusory person: a false self. This is the man that I want myself to be but who cannot exist, because God does not know anything about him.

For most of the people in the world, there is no greater subjective reality than this false self of theirs, which cannot exist.

All sin starts from the assumption that my false self, the self that exists only in my own egocentric desires, is the fundamental reality of life to which everything else in the universe is ordered.

I wind experiences around myself and cover myself with pleasures and glory like bandages in order to make myself perceptible to myself and to the world, as if I were an invisible body that could only become visible when something visible covered its surface.

The true depths of reality

The unknown remains unknown. It is still a mystery, for it cannot cease to be one. The function of faith is not to reduce mystery to rational clarity, but to integrate the unknown and the known together in a living whole, in which we are more and more able to transcend the limitations of our external self.

Faith is not just conformity, it is life. It embraces all the realms of life, penetrating into the most mysterious and inaccessible depths not only of our unknown spiritual being but even of God's own hidden essence and love.

Faith, then, is the only way of opening up the true depths of reality, even of our own reality.

Until a man yields himself to God in the consent of total belief, he must inevitably remain a stranger to himself, an exile from himself, because he is excluded from the most meaningful depths of his own being: those which remain obscure and unknown because they are too simple and too deep to be attained by reason.

Maturity

This power of self-surrender is not gained except through the experience of that dread which afflicts us when we taste the awful dereliction of the soul closed in upon itself.

The full maturity of the spiritual life cannot be reached unless we first pass through the dread, anguish, trouble and fear that necessarily accompany the inner crisis of 'spiritual death' in which we finally abandon our attachment to our exterior self and surrender completely to Christ.

But when this surrender has been truly made, there is no longer any place for fear and dread. There can no longer be any doubt or hesitation in the mind of one who is completely and finally resolved to seek nothing and do nothing but what is willed for him by God's love. 'Perfect love casts out dread', and dread itself is turned into love, confidence and hope.

The purpose of the dark night, as St John of the Cross shows, is not simply to punish and afflict the heart of man, but to liberate, to purify and to enlighten in perfect love. The way that leads through dread goes not to despair, but to perfect joy: not to hell, but to heaven.

Despair

Despair is the absolute extreme of self-love.

It is reached when a man deliberately turns his back on all help from anyone else in order to taste the rotten luxury of knowing himself to be lost.

In every man there is hidden some root of despair, because in every man there is pride that vegetates and springs weeds and rank flowers of self-pity as soon as our own resources fail us.

But because our own resources inevitably fail us, we are all more or less subject to discouragement and to despair.

Despair is the ultimate development of a pride so great and so stiff-necked that it selects the absolute misery of damnation rather than accept happiness from the hands of God and thereby acknowledge that He is above us and that we are not capable of fulfilling our destiny by ourselves.

But a man who is truly humble cannot despair, because in the humble man there is no longer any such thing as self-pity.

The key to faith

It is almost impossible to overestimate the value of true humility and its power in the spiritual life.

For the beginning of humility is the beginning of blessedness and the consummation of humility is the perfection of all joy.

Humility contains in itself the answer to all the great problems of the life of the soul. It is the only key to faith, with which the spiritual life begins: for faith and humility are inseparable.

In perfect humility all selfishness disappears and your soul no longer lives for itself: and it is lost and submerged in God and transformed into Him.

If we were incapable of humility we would be incapable of joy, because humility alone can destroy the self-centredness that makes joy impossible.

If there were no humility in the world, everybody would long ago have committed suicide.

Faith

Faith has to be something more than an assent of the mind. It is also a grasp, a contact, a communion of wills.

By faith one not only assents to propositions revealed by God, but one assents to God Himself. One receives God. One says 'yes' not merely to a statement about God, but to the Invisible, Infinite God Himself.

Faith is not just one moment of the spiritual life, not just a step to something else. It is that acceptance of God which is the very climate of all spiritual living. It is the beginning of communion.

I do not mean merely that now all our thoughts are couched in certain fideist or pietistic formulas, but rather that faith gives a dimension of simplicity and depth to all our apprehensions and to all our experiences.

What is this dimension of depth? It is the incorporation of the unknown and of the unconscious into our daily life. Faith brings together the known and the unknown so that they overlap: or, rather, so that we are aware of their overlapping.

Faith incorporates the unknown into our everyday life in a living, dynamic and actual manner.

The good choice

Reliance on God, of course, does not mean passivity. On the contrary, it liberates man for a clearly defined activity, 'the will of God'.

God wills that we act humanly, therefore intelligently. He wills that we act for His sake, for love of the truth, not out of concern for immediate material interest.

We find ourselves more and more backed into a corner in which there seems to be no choice but that of a 'lesser evil', for the sake of some urgency, some imaginary or desperately hoped-for good. But an evil choice can never have wholly good consequences. When one chooses to do good irrespective of the consequences, it is a paradox that the consequences will ultimately be good.

We are not responsible for more than our own action, but for this we should take complete responsibility. Then the results will follow of themselves, in a manner we may not always be able to foresee. We do not always have to foresee every possibility.

We must recover our inner faith not only in God but in the good . . . in the power of the good to take care of itself and us as well.

To be possessed

God is invisibly present to the ground of our being, but he remains hidden from the arrogant gaze of our investigating mind which seeks to capture him and secure permanent possession of him in an act of knowledge.

In seeking to know him we must forget the familiar subject–object relationship which characterizes our ordinary acts of knowing. Instead we know him in so far as we become aware of ourselves as known through and through by him.

We 'possess' him in proportion as we realize ourselves to be possessed by him in the inmost depths of our being. The aim of meditation is to come to know him through the realization that our very being is penetrated with his knowledge and love for us.

We have no other reason for being, except to be loved by him as our Creator and Redeemer, and to love him in return.

The whole purpose of meditation is to deepen the consciousness of this basic relationship of the creature to the Creator, and of the sinner to his Redeemer.

My own nothingness

It is not enough to turn away in disgust from my illusions and faults and mistakes, to separate myself from them as if they were not, and as if I were someone other than myself. This kind of self-annihilation is only a worse illusion; it is a pretended humility which, by saying 'I am nothing', I mean in effect 'I wish I were not what I am'.

This can flow from an experience of our deficiencies and of our helplessness, but it does not produce any peace in us.

To really know our 'nothingness' we must also love it. And we cannot love it unless we see that it is good. And we cannot see that it is good unless we accept it.

A supernatural experience of our contingency is humility which loves and prizes above all else our state of moral and metaphysical helplessness before God.

To love our 'nothingness' in this way, we must repudiate nothing that is our own, nothing that we have, nothing that we are. We must see and admit that it is all ours and that it is all good: . . . since our helplessness, even our moral misery, attracts to us the mercy of God.

The wasteland

The Desert Fathers believed that the wilderness had been created as supremely valuable in the eyes of God precisely because it had no value to men.

The wasteland was the land that could never be wasted by men because it offered them nothing. There was nothing to attract them. There was nothing to exploit.

The desert was the region in which the Chosen People had wandered for forty years, cared for by God alone. They could have reached the Promised Land in a few months if they had travelled directly to it.

God's plan was that they should learn to love Him in the wilderness and that they should always look back upon the time in the desert as the idyllic time of their life with Him alone.

The desert was created simply to be itself, not to be transformed by men into something else.

The desert is therefore the logical dwelling-place for the man who seeks to be nothing but himself – that is to say, a creature solitary and poor and dependent upon no one but God, with no great project standing between himself and his Creator.

The goodness of all things

The further I advance into solitude the more clearly I see the goodness of all things.

In order to live happily in solitude I must have a compassionate knowledge of the goodness of other men, a reverent knowledge of the goodness of all creation and a humble knowledge of the goodness of my own body and of my own soul.

How can I live in solitude if I do not see everywhere the goodness of God, my Creator and Redeemer and the Father of all good?

What is it that has made me evil and hateful to myself? It is my own folly, my own darkness, which have divided me, by sin, against the light which God has placed in my soul to be the reflection of His goodness and the witness of His mercy.

Shall I drive evil out of my soul by wrestling with my own darkness? This is not what God has planned for me.

It is sufficient to turn away from my darkness to His light. I do not have to run away from myself; it is sufficient that I find myself, not as I have made myself, by my own stupidity, but as He has made me in His wisdom and remade me in His infinite mercy.

Being and doing

The fact that our being necessarily demands to be expressed in action should not lead us to believe that as soon as we stop acting we cease to exist.

We do not live merely in order to 'do something' – no matter what. We do not live more fully merely by doing more, seeing more, tasting more, and experiencing more than we ever have before.

Everything depends on the quality of our acts and our experiences. A multitude of badly performed actions and of experiences only half-lived exhausts and depletes our being.

By doing things badly we make ourselves less real. This growing unreality cannot help but make us unhappy and fill us with a sense of guilt.

There are times, then, when in order to keep ourselves in existence at all we simply have to sit back for a while and do nothing. And for a man who has let himself be drawn completely out of himself by his activity, nothing is more difficult than to sit still and rest, doing nothing at all.

We must first recover the possession of our own being before we can act wisely or taste any experience in its reality.

Authenticity

Man is not himself. He has lost himself in the falsities and illusions of a massive organization. How can he recover his authenticity and his true identity? What is meant by identity?

For practical purposes here we are talking about one's own authentic and personal beliefs and convictions, based on experience of oneself as a person, experience of one's ability to choose and reject even good things which are not relevant to one's own life.

One does not receive 'identity' in this sense along with life and vegetative existence. To have identity is not merely to have a face and a name, a recognizable physical presence. Identity in this deep sense is something that one must create for oneself by choices that are significant and that require a courageous commitment in the face of anguish and risk.

This means much more than just having an address and a name in the telephone book. It means having a belief one stands by; it means having certain definite ways of responding to life, of meeting its demands, of loving other people, and in the last analysis, of serving God.

In this sense, identity is one's witness to truth in one's life.

True liberation

The beginning of the fight against hatred, the basic Christian answer to hatred, is not the commandment to love, but what must necessarily come before in order to make the commandment bearable and comprehensible.

It is a prior commandment to believe. The root of Christian love is not the will to love, but the faith that one is loved by God. That faith that one is loved by God although unworthy or, rather, irrespective of one's worth!

In the true Christian vision of God's love, the idea of worthiness loses its significance. Revelation of the mercy of God makes the whole problem of worthiness something almost laughable: the discovery that worthiness is of no special consequence (since no one could ever, by himself, be strictly worthy to be loved with such a love) is a true liberation of the spirit.

And until this discovery is made, until this liberation has been brought about by the divine mercy, man is imprisoned in hate.

At Gethsemani

It seems to me the most absurd thing in the world to be upset because I am weak and distracted and blind and constantly make mistakes! What else do I expect!

Does God love me any less because I can't make myself a saint by my own power and in my own way? He loves me more because I am so clumsy and helpless without Him – and underneath what I am He sees me as I will one day be by His pure gift and that pleases Him – and therefore it pleases me and I attend to His great love which is my joy.

Yesterday Father Macarius and I went out and blessed the fields, starting with the wheat and oats and coming around by St Bernard's field and Aidan Nally's and across to the bottoms.

Out in the calf pasture we blessed some calves who came running up and took a very active interest in everything. Then we blessed pigs, who showed some interest at first. The sheep showed no concern and the chickens ran away as soon as we approached.

The rabbits stayed quiet until we threw holy water at them and then they all jumped.

Vigil of the Ascension

Last night there were thunderstorms: but today everything is beautiful. The leaves on the hickory tree by the cemetery are small and the flowers fill the branches with fringes of green lace. I hear the engine running down at the mill: only that, and the birds singing.

Tomorrow is the Ascension, my favourite feast. At any time in the year I am liable to find the antiphons of Ascension Day ringing in my ears and they fill me with light and peace. 'I go to prepare a place for you.'

It is the feast of silence and interior solitude when we go up to live in heaven with Jesus: for He takes us there, after He has lived a little while on earth among us.

That is the grace of Ascension Day: to be taken up into the heaven of our own souls, the point of immediate contact with God. To rest on this quiet peak, in the darkness that surrounds God. To live there through all trials and all business with the 'tranquil God Who makes all things tranquil'.

God be with me this day and forever.

My conversion

I think that, like most other converts, I faced the
problem of the 'religiousness' and came to terms
with it.

God was not for me a working hypothesis, to fill
in gaps left open by a scientific world-view. Nor
was He a God enthroned somewhere in outer
space. Nor did I ever feel any particular 'need' for
superficial religious routines merely to keep myself
happy. I would even say that, like most modern
men, I have not been much moved by the concept
of 'getting into heaven' after muddling through
this present life.

On the contrary, my conversion to Catholicism
began with the realization of the presence of God
in this present life, in the world and in myself, and
that my task as a Christian is to live in full and
vital awareness of this ground of my being and of
the world's being.

Acts and forms of worship help one to do this,
and the Church, with her liturgy and sacraments,
gives us the essential means of grace. Yet God can
work without these means if He so wills.

When I entered the Church I came seeking God,
the living God, and not just 'the consolations of
religion'.

Courage in prayer

Sooner or later, if we follow Christ we have to risk everything in order to gain everything.

We have to gamble on the invisible and risk all that we can see and taste and feel. But we know the risk is worth it, because there is nothing more insecure than the transient world.

Without courage we can never attain to true simplicity.

Cowardice keeps us 'double-minded' – hesitating between the world and God. In this hesitation, there is no true faith – faith remains an opinion. We are never certain, because we never quite give in to the authority of an invisible God.

This hesitation is the death of hope. We never let go of those visible supports which, we well know, must one day surely fail us.

And this hesitation makes true prayer impossible – it never quite dares to ask for anything, or if it asks, it is so uncertain of being heard that in the very act of asking it surreptitiously seeks, by human prudence, to construct a makeshift answer.

What is the use of praying if at the very moment of prayer we have so little confidence in God that we are busy planning our own kind of answer to our prayer?

The purpose of meditation

Recollection is awareness of the unconditional. Prayer then means yearning for the simple presence of God. Our desire and our prayer should be summed up in St Augustine's words: May I know you, may I know myself.

We wish to gain a true evaluation of ourselves and of the world so as to understand the meaning of our life as children of God redeemed from sin and death. We wish to gain a true loving knowledge of God, our Father and Redeemer. We wish to lose ourselves in his love and rest in him. We wish to hear his word and respond to it with our whole being.

We wish to know his merciful will and submit to it in its totality.

All prayer, reading, meditation and all the activities of the monastic life are aimed at purity of heart, an unconditional and totally humble surrender to God, a total acceptance of ourselves and of our situation as willed by him.

It means the renunciation of all deluded images of ourselves, all exaggerated estimates of our own capacities, in order to obey God's will as it comes to us in the difficult demands of life in its exacting truth.

Learn to trust God

It would be sentimental folly to expect men to trust one another when they obviously cannot be trusted. But at least they can learn to trust God.

They can bring themselves to see that the mysterious power of God can protect men unaccountably against themselves, and that He can always turn evil into good.

If they can trust and love God, who is infinitely wise and who rules the lives of men, permitting them to use their freedom even to the point of almost incredible abuse, they can love men who are evil.

If we can love the men we cannot trust and if we can to some extent share the burden of their sin by identifying ourselves with them, then perhaps there is some hope of a kind of peace on earth, based not on the wisdom and the manipulations of men but on the inscrutable mercy of God.

For only love – which means humility – can exorcize the fear which is at the root of all war.

The world must burn

Sooner or later the world must burn, and all things in it – all the books, the cloister together with the brothel, Fra Angelico together with the Lucky Strike ads. Sooner or later it will all be consumed by fire and nobody will be left.

But love laughs at the end of the world because love is the door to eternity and he who loves God is playing on the doorstep of eternity, and before anything can happen love will have drawn him over the sill and closed the door and he won't bother about the world burning because he will know nothing but love.

I have several times thought how at the Last Day I am likely to be one of the ten most abjectly humiliated sinners in the history of the world, but it will be my joy, and it will fill me with love, and I will fly like an arrow to take a back seat very far in the back where the last shall be first.

And perhaps if St Francis will pray for me, and St John of the Cross, and St Mary Magdalene, I'll slide down off my high horse now and begin being the last and least in everything.

The office of the monk

The office of the monk or the marginal person, the meditative person or the poet, is to go beyond death even in this life, to go beyond the dichotomy of life and death and to be, therefore, a witness to life.

This requires, of course, faith, but as soon as you say faith in terms of this monastic and marginal existence you run into another problem. Faith means doubt. Faith is not the suppression of doubt. It is the overcoming of doubt, and you overcome doubt by going through it.

The man of faith who has never experienced doubt is not a man of faith. Consequently, the monk is one who has to struggle in the depths of his being with the presence of doubt, to break through beyond doubt into a certitude which is very, very deep . . . it is the certitude of God Himself, in us.

The only ultimate reality is God. God lives and dwells in us. We are called by the voice of God, by the voice of that ultimate being, to pierce through the irrelevance of our life, while accepting and admitting that our life is totally irrelevant, in order to find relevance in Him.

The higher freedom

The Holy Spirit comes to set the whole house of our soul in order, to deliver our minds from immaturity, alienation, fear and tenacious prejudice.

If Christ is the Lamb of God Who takes away the sins of the world, then surely He sends His Spirit to deliver our souls from obsession with our feelings of guilt.

This is the thing so many Christians refuse to see. They think Christ's power to deliver us from sin is not a real liberation but an assertion of His own rights over us. The truth is that it is both, for when God asserts 'His rights' over us we become free. God is Truth and 'the truth shall make you free'.

This is precisely what we fail to understand. With respect to the higher freedom of grace, our natural freedom is simply a potency waiting to be developed.

It is paradoxically by the grace of God that we finally achieve our full spiritual freedom and it is a gift of God that enables us to stand on our own feet.

The thief Prometheus

Far from killing the man who seeks the divine fire, the Living God will Himself pass through death in order that man may have what is destined for him.

If Christ has died and risen from the dead and poured out upon us the fire of His Holy Spirit, why do we imagine that our desire for life is a Promethean desire, doomed to punishment?

Why do we act as if our longing to 'see good days' were something God did not desire, when He Himself told us to seek them? Why do we reproach ourselves for desiring victory? Why do we pride ourselves on our defeats, and glory in despair?

Because we think our life is important to ourselves alone, and do not know that our life is more important to the Living God than it is to our own selves.

Because we think our happiness is for ourselves alone, and do not realize that it is also His happiness. Because we think our sorrows are for ourselves alone, and do not believe that they are much more than that: they are His sorrows.

There is nothing we can steal from Him at all, because before we can think of stealing it, it has already been given.

Winter

Meadow larks singing in the snow, along the road from the cow barns. Icy water of the running stream, full of sun, flowing over green watercress between banks of snow.

Dark blue water of the lake, edged with melting ice and snow.

Evening: cold winter wind along the walls of the chapel. Not howling, not moaning, not dismal. Can there be anything mournful about wind? It is innocent, and without sorrow. It has no regrets.

Wind is a strong child enjoying his play, amazed at his own strength, gentle, inexhaustible, and pure. He burnishes the dry snow, throwing clouds of it against the building. The wind has no regrets.

The chapel is very cold. Two die-hard novices remain there alone, kneeling both upright, very still, no longer even pretending to enjoy or to understand anything.

We must face the fact

In order to face suffering in peace: Suffer without imposing on others a theory of suffering ... without proclaiming yourself a martyr, without counting out the price of your courage, without disdaining sympathy and without seeking too much of it.

We must be sincere in our sufferings as in anything else. We must recognize at once our weakness and our pain, but we do not need to advertise them. We must face the fact that it is much harder to stand the long monotony of slight suffering than a passing onslaught of intense pain.

In either case, what is hard is our own poverty, and the spectacle of our own selves reduced more and more to nothing, wasting away in our own estimation and in that of our friends. We must be willing to accept also the bitter truth that, in the end, we may have to become a burden to those who love us.

But it is necessary that we face this also. It takes heroic charity and humility to let others sustain us when we are absolutely incapable of sustaining ourselves.

We cannot suffer well unless we see Christ everywhere – both in suffering and in the charity of those who come to the aid of our affliction.

Your child and your friend

Here you ask of me nothing else than to be content that I am your child and your friend. Which means simply to accept your friendship because it is your friendship, and your Fatherhood because I am your son.

You have called me here to be repeatedly born in the Spirit as your son: to speak your name of 'Father' just by being here as 'son' in the Spirit and the Light which you have given, and which are no unearthly light but simply this plain June day, with its shining fields, its tulip tree, the pines, the woods, the clouds, and the flowers everywhere.

To be here with the silence of sonship in my heart is to be a centre in which all things converge upon you. That is surely enough for the time being.

Therefore, Father, I beg you to keep me in this silence so that I may learn from it the word of your peace and the word of your mercy and the word of your gentleness to the world: and that through me perhaps your word of peace may make itself heard where it has not been possible for anyone to hear it for a long time.

God's love

It is God's love that warms me in the sun and God's love that sends the cold rain. It is God's love that feeds me in the bread I eat and God that feeds me also by hunger and fasting.

It is the love of God that sends the winter days when I am cold and sick, and the hot summer when I labour and my clothes are full of sweat: but it is God who breathes on me with light winds off the river and in the breezes out of the wood.

His love spreads the shade of the sycamore over my head and sends the water-boy along the edge of the wheat field with a bucket from the spring, while the labourers are resting and the mules stand under the tree.

It is God's love that speaks to me in the birds and streams; but also behind the clamour of the city God speaks to me in His judgments, and all of these things are seeds sent to me from His will.

My food is the will of Him who made me and who made all things in order to give Himself to me through them.

Sources and Index

The editor wishes to thank these publishers for permission to use excerpts from the following books:

Farrar Straus & Giroux Inc. *Thoughts in Solitude* © 1956, 1958 by the Abbey of Gethsemani; renewed 1986; *Love and Living* © 1965, 1966, 1968, 1969, 1977, 1979 by Trustees of the Merton Legacy Trust; *The New Man* © 1961 by The Abbey of Gethsemani; *Seeds of Destruction* © 1961, 1962, 1963, 1964 by the Abbey of Gethsemani.

New Directions Publishing Co. *Asian Journal* © 1973 by the Abbey of Gethsemani; *New Seeds of Contemplation* © 1961 by the Abbey of Gethsemani; *Raids on the Unspeakable* © 1966 by the Abbey of Gethsemani.

Harcourt Brace Jovanovich Inc. *No Man Is An Island* © 1955 by the Abbey of Gethsemani, renewed 1983 by the Trustees of the Merton Legacy Trust; *The Sign of Jonas* © 1953 by the Abbey of Gethsemani, renewed 1981 by Trustees of the Merton Legacy Trust.

The Liturgical Press, Collegeville MN *Spiritual Direction and Meditation* © 1960.

Bantam Doubleday Dell Publishing Group Inc. *Contemplation in a World of Action* © 1973 by the Abbey of Gethsemani; *Conjectures of a Guilty Bystander* © 1966 by the Abbey of Gethsemani.

Cistercian Publications *The Climate of Monastic Prayer* © 1969.

Abbreviations used in source references: AJ Asian Journal, CGB Conjectures of a Guilty Bystander, CMP Climate of Monastic Prayer, CWA Contemplation in a World of Action, LL Love and Living, NM The New Man, NMI No Man Is An Island, NSC New Seeds of Contemplation, SD Seeds of Destruction, RU Raids on the Unspeakable, SDM Spiritual Direction and Meditation, SJ The Sign of Jonas, TS Thoughts in Solitude. The figures in bold type refer to the pages of Readings in this book. They are followed by the sources.

23	*AJ* appendix ix	57	*NSC* ch.6
24	*NMI* ch. 6; 7; 10	58	*NSC* ch.1
25	*NMI* ch. 6; 15	59	*NSC* ch.5
26	*SJ* part 6	60	*NSC* ch. 19
27	*SJ* part 5	61	*CMP* ch. 18
28	*SJ* part 5	62	*NSC* ch. 25
29	*LL* ch. 3, sect. 1	65	*NSC* ch. 25
30	*SD* 1 (5); 2 (5)	66	*NSC* ch. 19
31	*LL* ch. 1, sect. 2	67	*CGB* part 2
32	*NMI* ch. 4-10	68	*CMP* ch. 14
33	*NSC* ch. 4	69	*TS* ch. 9
34	*SD* ch. 6	70	*TS* ch. 1
37	*SD* ch. 6	71	*SDM* p. 115
38	*CWA* ch. 5	72	*NMI* ch. 7; 4
39	*CMP* ch. 4	73	*CWA* ch. 3
40	*CGB* part 3	74	*NSC* ch. 10
41	*CGB* part 5	75	*SJ* part 2
42	*NSC* ch. 5	76	*SJ* part 1
43	*NM* part 1, 32	79	*CGB* part 5
44	*NM* part 1, 33	80	*TS* ch.5
45	*CGB* part 3	81	*CMP* ch. 11
46	*SDM* ch. 5 (2)	82	*NSC* ch. 16
47	*NM* part 1, 64	83	*SJ* part 2
48	*NMI* ch. 10, 14	84	*AJ* appendix iii
51	*CMP* ch. 16	85	*NM* part 1, 28
52	*CMP* ch. 18	86	*RU* ch. 6
53	*SJ* part 5	87	*CGB* pp. 19-20
54	*NSC* ch. 39	88	*NMI* ch. 5; 17
55	*NSC* ch. 5; 6	89	*CGB* part 3
56	*NSC* ch. 5	90	*NSC* ch. 3